Moon Cakes

A traditional story retold by
Lee Choon-Yi
Art by Vladimir Aleksic

Literacy Consultants
David Booth • Kathleen Corrigan

Contents

Chapter 1

The Moon Festival Legend

"What are these round cakes, Papa?" asked Jolene.

"They are moon cakes," said Papa. "We eat them during the Moon Festival."

"But why, Papa?" asked Jolene.

"Let me tell you the story about moon cakes," said Papa.

"Long, long ago, a group of people called the Mongols invaded China. They were cruel to the Chinese. Mongol guards were everywhere. The Chinese people had to obey the Mongols," explained Papa.

"Life became very hard for the Chinese people.
They had to pay taxes to the Mongols.
Some rebels tried to overthrow the Mongol rulers.
But these rebels all failed," said Papa.

"Many hard years passed.
At last, a young man named Zhu became
the leader of the rebels.
Zhu and his rebels planned an attack.
They would attack the Mongols on the
fifteenth night of the eighth month.
There would be a full moon that night,"
said Papa.

"Zhu knew that he needed the help of all the Chinese villagers.
But how would he spread the message?
Mongol guards were everywhere.
At last, Zhu came up with a good plan," continued Papa.

Chapter 2

Zhu's Plan

"Zhu asked the rebels to bake lots and lots of moon cakes," said Papa. "They put a message inside each cake.

The message read 'Overthrow the Mongols. We will attack on the fifteenth night of the eighth month.'"

"That's so clever!" said Jolene.

"Do you want to find out what happened next?" asked Papa.

"Yes! Keep going!" cried Jolene.

Papa continued the story.

"A few nights before the attack, the rebels went from house to house. They gave each family a moon cake."

"A moon cake? Why?" asked Jolene.

"The rebels told the villagers to open the moon cakes and eat them.
So when all the villagers split open their moon cakes, they found the secret message hidden inside.
They knew what they had to do," explained Papa.

Chapter 3

The Surprise Attack

"The villagers were careful.
They kept the plan to themselves.
On the night of the full moon, the rebels and villagers gathered together.
They were able to surprise the Mongols.
The rebels and villagers defeated them.
The Mongols were driven out of China," said Papa.

"Thanks to Zhu and his rebels, the Chinese people were finally free. Later, Zhu became the first emperor of the Ming Dynasty," said Papa.

"That is such a cool story, Papa," said Jolene.

"The story has been passed down for many years," explained Papa. "Today, Chinese people around the world celebrate the mid-Autumn Festival, or Moon Festival, with their own moon cakes."

"In the past, moon cakes were filled with lotus paste," said Papa.
"Today, people make them with different kinds of fillings.

But the Chinese still remember the overthrow of the Mongols as they eat the moon cakes. It's an important piece of history."

"Wow! So cool, Dad!" said Jolene.

"All of that moon cake talk has made me hungry. What about you?
Let's have some moon cakes!" said Papa.

Mama walked in carrying a big plate.

"The moon cakes are cut and ready for eating. Dig in!" cried Mama.

"You know, Papa," said Jolene.
"If there had been the Internet back then,
Zhu and his rebels would not have needed
moon cakes to spread their message."

"You're right," said Papa.
Then he took a bite of moon cake.
"But moon cakes are tastier than
the Internet!"